VICTORIAN STAINED GLASS PATTERN BOOK

96 DESIGNS FOR WORKABLE PROJECTS

Ed Sibbett, Jr.

DOVER PUBLICATIONS, INC.
NEW YORK

Victorian Stained Glass Pattern Book is a new work, first published by Dover Publications, Inc., in 1979.

DOVER *Pictorial Archive* SERIES

International Standard Book Number: 0-486-23811-3
Library of Congress Catalog Card Number: 79-52351

Manufactured in the United States of America
Dover Publications, Inc.
31 East 2nd Street, Mineola, N.Y. 11501

PUBLISHER'S NOTE

One of the glories of the Victorian house—be it a modest frame cottage or an imposing stone edifice—was the stained glass work adorning its windows, doors, transoms, fanlights, room screens, lampshades and dozens of other household objects. Generally executed in rich hues of blue, red, green and gold, these luminous decorations were the perfect complement to the grace and dignity of the Victorian dwelling.

Mr. Sibbett's inspiration for this collection of designs has come from numerous style and pattern books of the last half of the nineteenth century as well as from Victorian stained glass objects that he has been able to examine, often in their original settings. His drawings maintain the wonderful balance between the semi-stylized plant and floral motifs and the geometric backgrounds that is characteristically Victorian.

A useful feature of this collection is that several double-page spreads are devoted to presenting variations on themes: a distinctive motif executed, for instance, in a square or nearly square block and/or a narrow rectangle, a circle, semicircle, oval, etc. Experienced craftsmen will be able to adapt other designs in a similar fashion, to achieve virtually any shape desired.

The 96 patterns in this anthology are suitable for a wide variety of craft projects—windows, lampshades, mirrors, ornaments, mobiles, etc. Suppliers of glass and other materials, including general instruction books and tools for the beginner, should be listed in your local Yellow Pages.

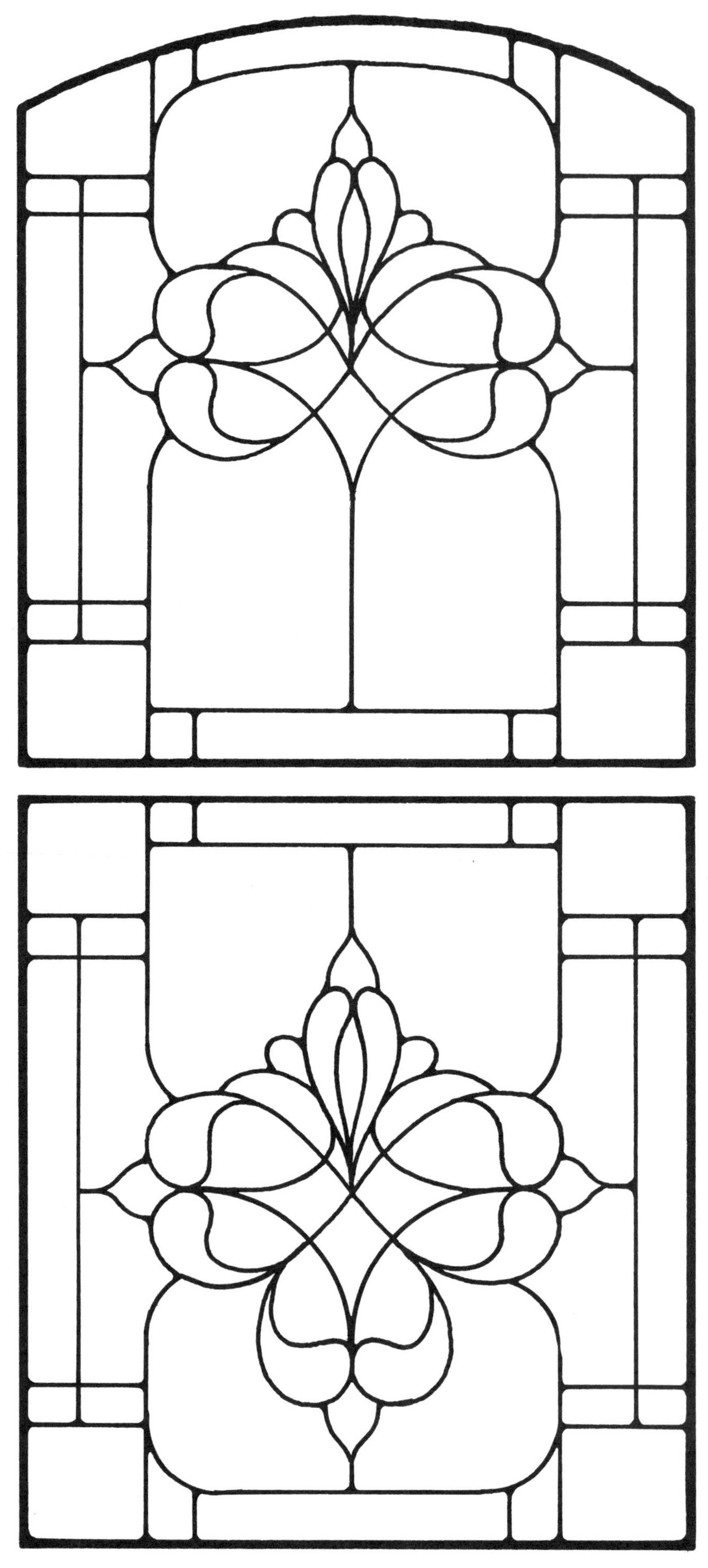

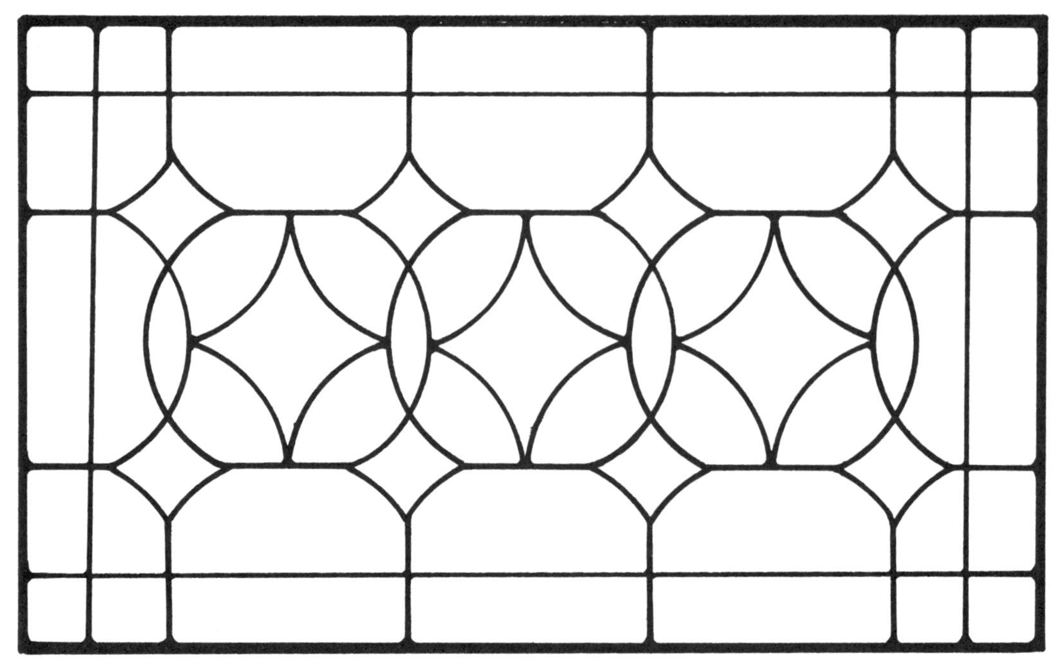

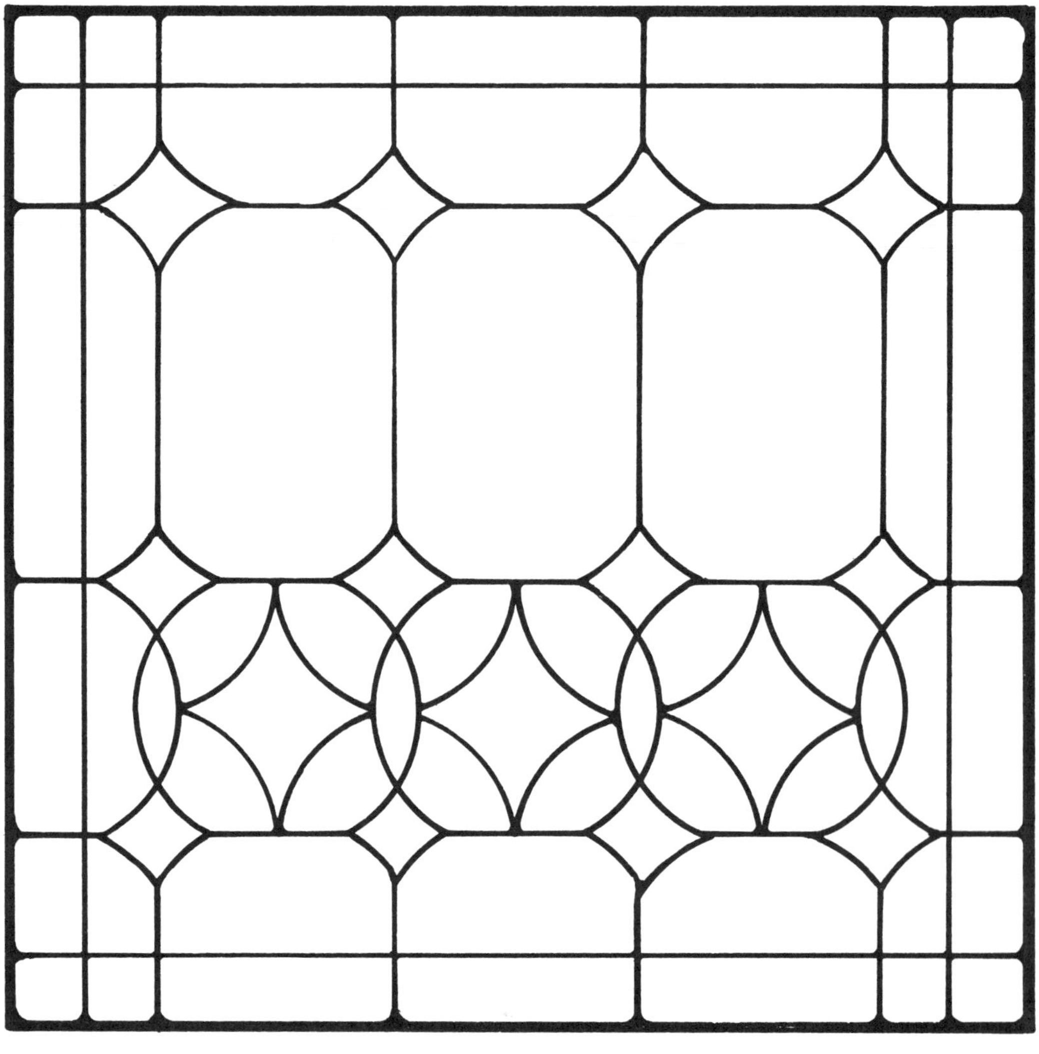

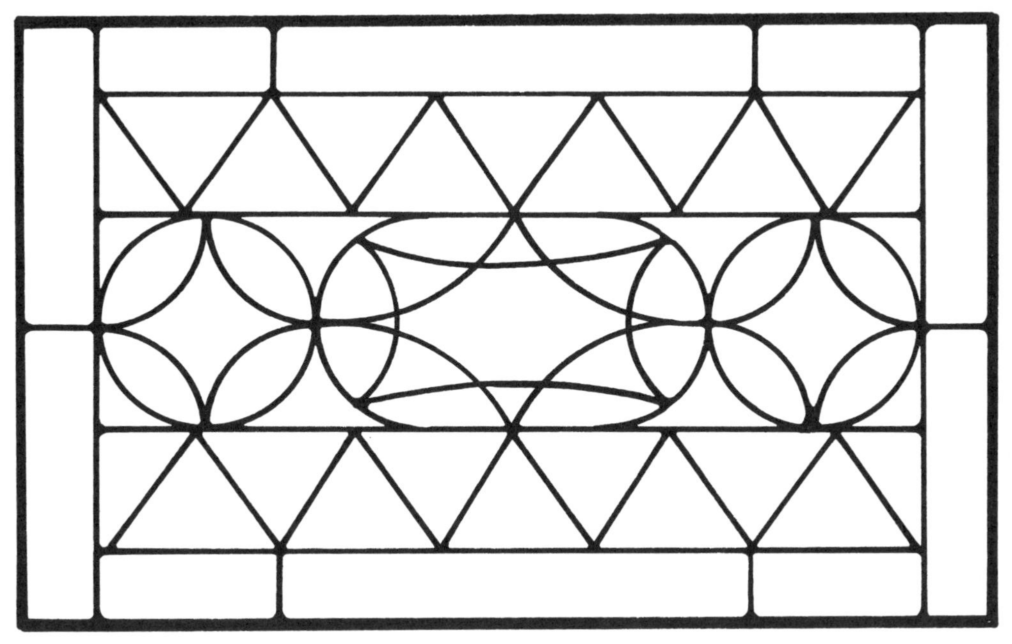

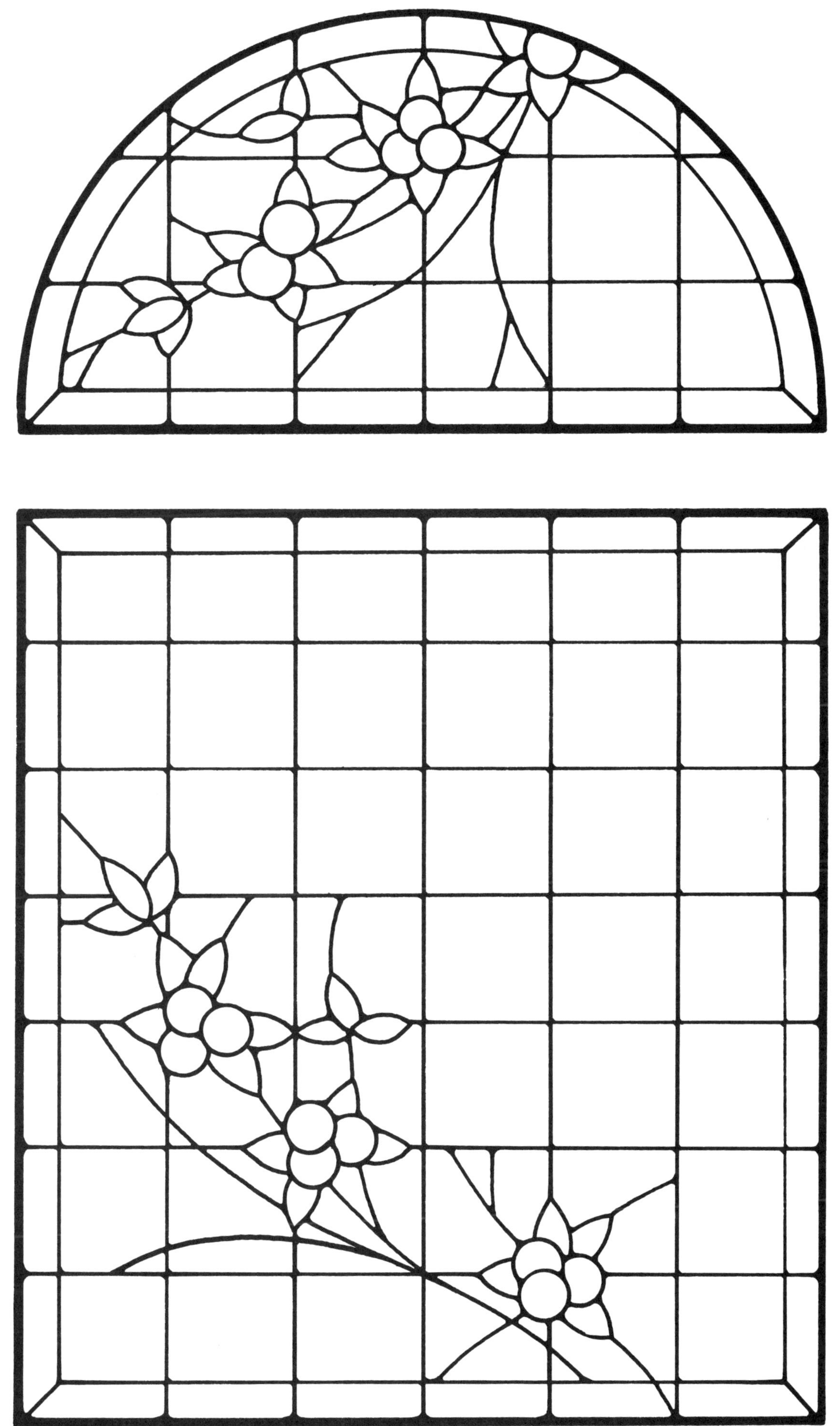

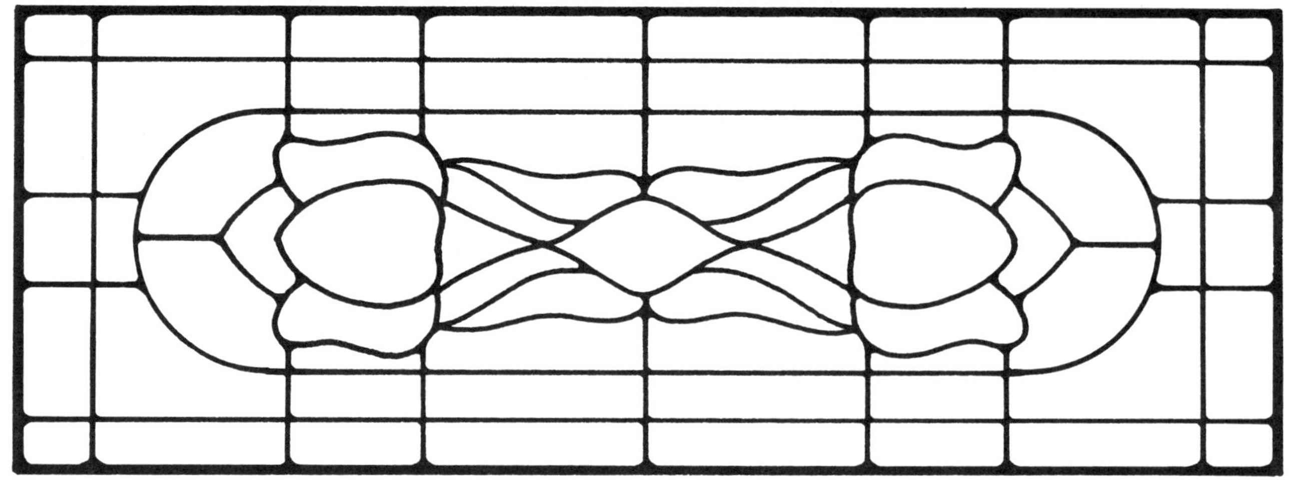

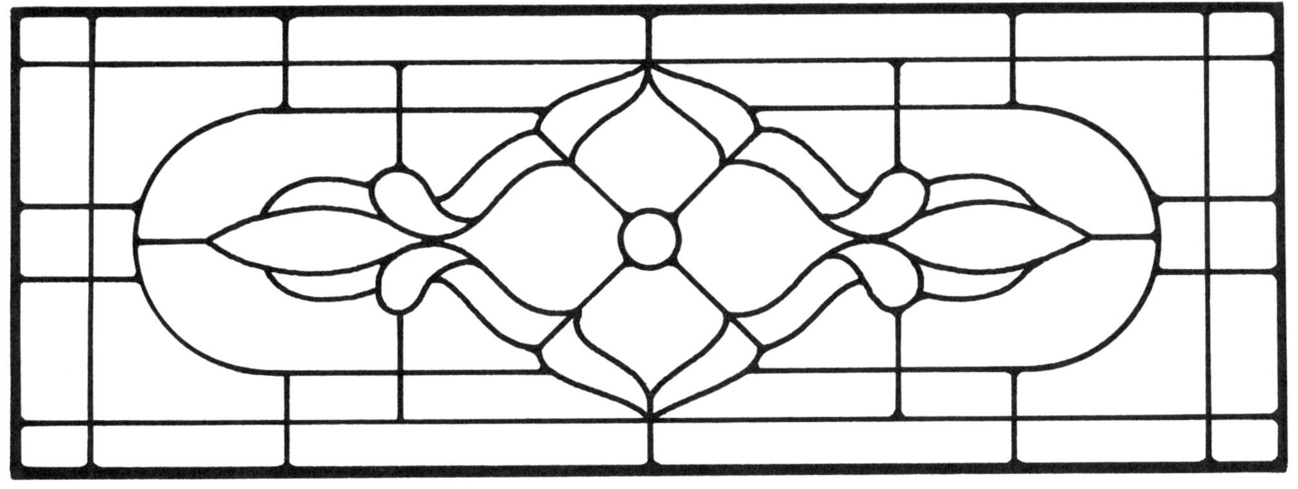

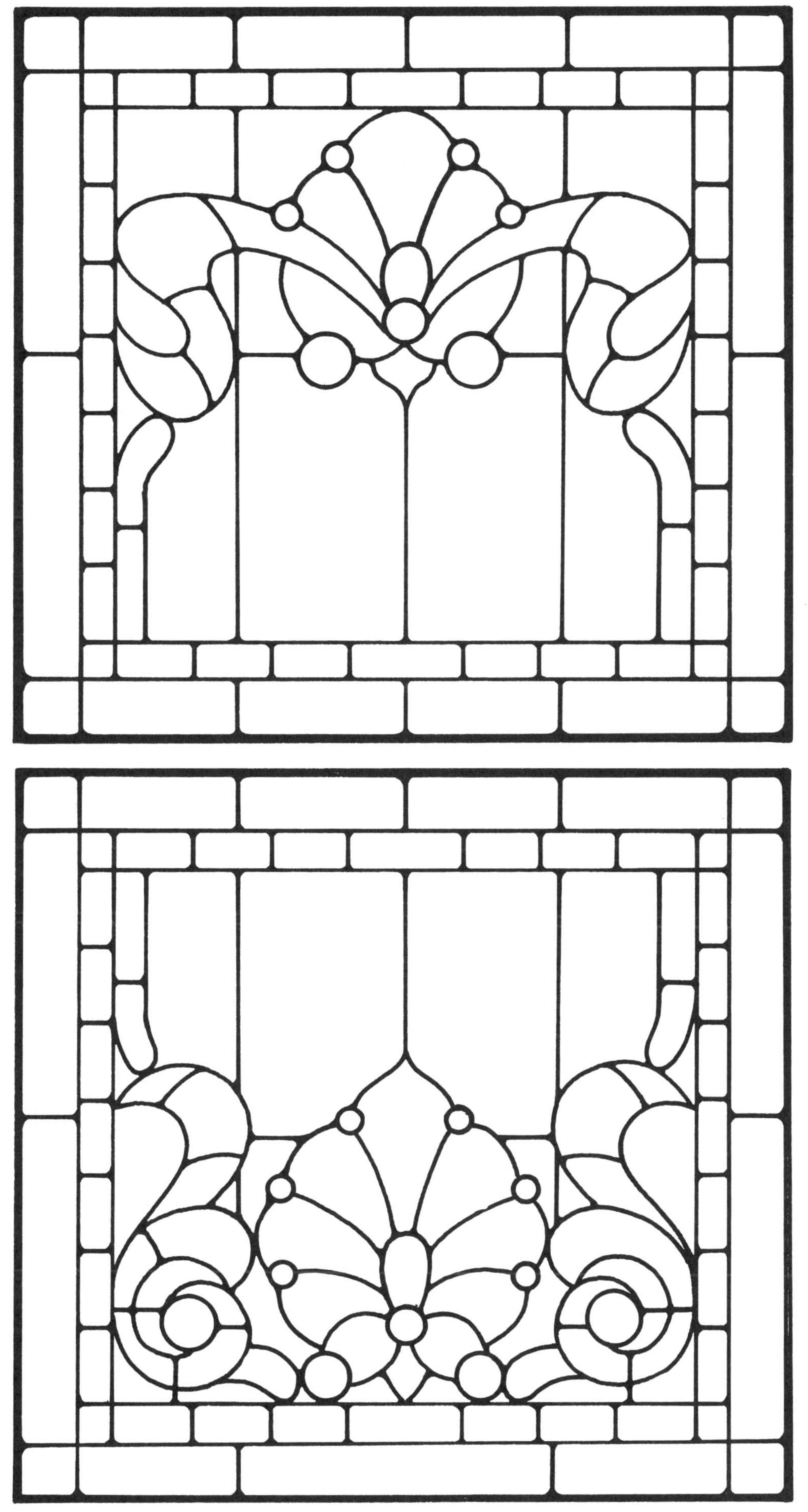

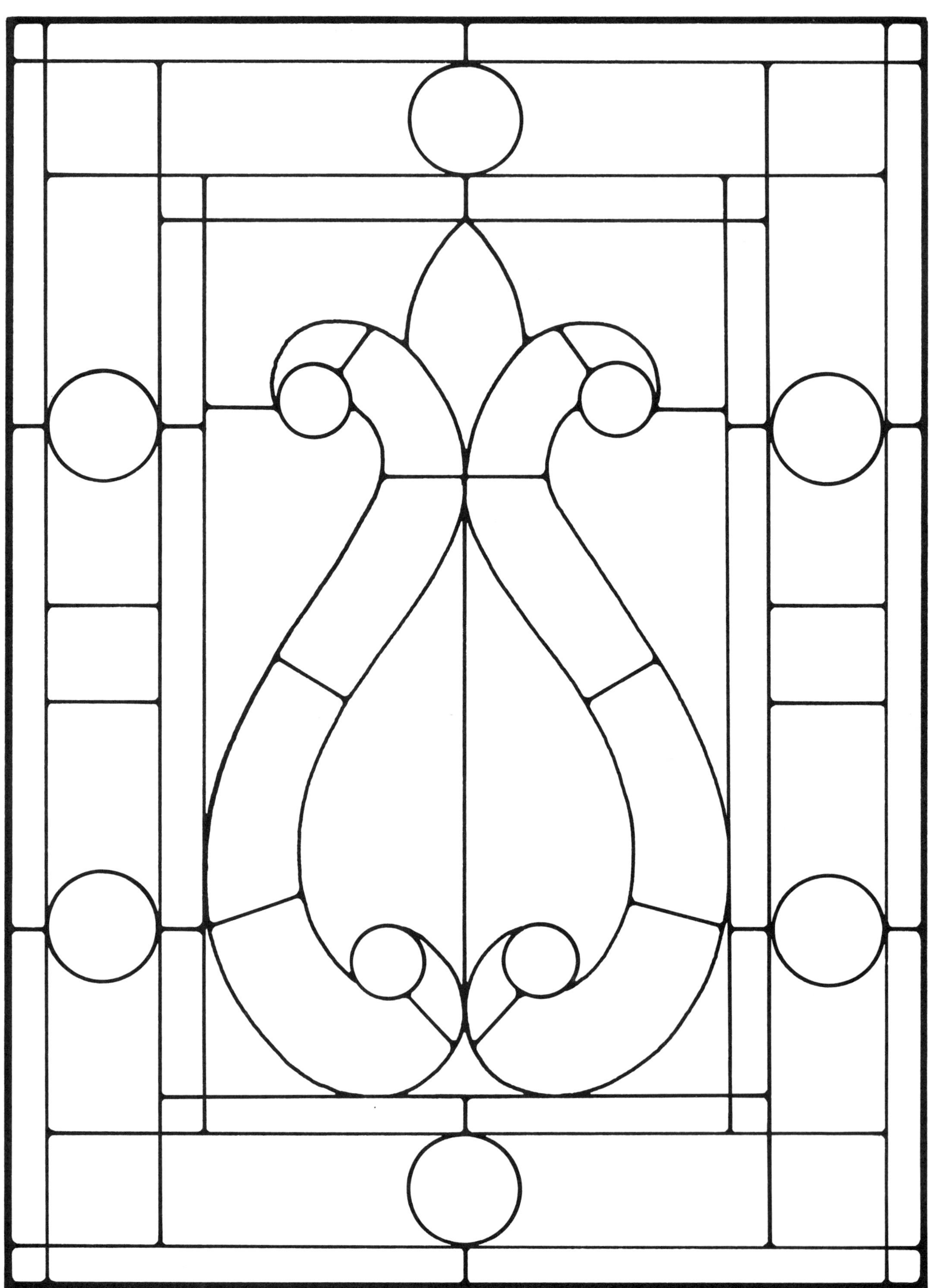